Lokmanya Tilak

SYMBOL OF SWARAJ

Sorab Ghaswalla

Rupa & Co

Published in 2003 by
Rupa . Co

7/16, Ansari Road, Daryaganj
New Delhi 110 002

Sales Centres:
Allahabad Bangalore Chandigarh Chennai
Hyderabad Jaipur Kathmandu
Kolkata Ludhiana Mumbai Pune

Cover & Book Design by
Arrt Creations
45 Nehru Apts, Kalkaji
New Delhi 110 019

Printed in India by
International Print-o-Pac Ltd.
B-204, 205, 206, Okhla Industrial Area,
Phase-I, New Delhi-20

CONTENTS

True Nationalist

Born July 23, 1856

(Died August 1, 1920)

A single word cannot accurately describe Bal Gangadhar Tilak's persona. Some historians have called Tilak, the 'uncrowned' King of India. If he had been alive today, Tilak would have smiled at the irony in this description. For, most of his adult life was spent fighting British sovereignty in India.

Was he a patriot who was more successful in his attempts than others, in rousing the people of India against the British rule? Or like his official biographer D.V. Tahmankar puts it — was Tilak to India what George Washington was to the United States of America? So, was he a 'nation maker'?

Let us look at what Mahatma Gandhi, known for his astute sense of observation, had to say about the Lokmanya while paying homage to him, “His patriotism was a passion with him. He knew no religion but love for his country. He was a born democrat…” Gandhi himself labelled the Lokmanya as the ‘maker of modern India.’

Several Tilak-era scholars and researchers have tried tagging various labels on the Lokmanya. Some have called him a revolutionary, some say he was a social activist, yet for others, he was a true nationalist. Some have even called him an ‘extremist’ in thought. History shows that Tilak was all this and much more. So, try as we may, the Lokmanya just cannot be neatly compartmentalised.

India and its future were dear to Tilak. No doubt, he was aware that some people often called him a ‘hard liner’. But Tilak was a man ahead of his times. His actions, his words, were sometimes misjudged by his contemporaries. Often, they criticised him for some of his actions, only to be proven wrong in hindsight.

There were some facets of Tilak’s personality that were never really fully understood. In fact, more often than not, they were misread, deliberately or otherwise. Critics those days had labelled Tilak a ‘reactionary to social reform’, and even ‘anti-Muslim’.

When Hindu-Muslim riots broke out in Bombay and Pune in 1893, Tilak criticised the British government’s bi-partisan attitude towards Hindu-Muslim relations. He accused them of practising the policy of ‘divide and rule’. But the Lokmanya also made it abundantly clear that he was not against the Muslims *per se* but against this ‘heinous’ political ploy of the British.

Tilak was the first national leader from Maharashtra, and remained a true nationalist. Nobody ever doubted his nationalistic fervour. All his political life, he stood by his legendary slogan, ‘Swaraj is my birth right and I shall have it’. It is also unanimously agreed that the Lokmanya was the ‘father of Indian unrest’.

Lokmanya Tilak at his study desk in Poona.

The Lokmanya would have scaled more heights of fame had it not been for his untimely death in August 1920, just when the Indian freedom struggle was gaining momentum. But the visionary that he was, Tilak, with his ideas like self-rule and self-reliance, had paved the way for later day leaders to walk down the path.

It was Tilak's mantra of *swadeshi* (self-reliance) which was later picked up by 'Bapu' (Mahatma Gandhi) and taken to its logical conclusion. Besides *swadeshi,* Tilak tried to rouse a moribund nation through his three other mantras — the boycott of foreign goods, national education and self-government.

Compared to his sterling role in India's freedom struggle, not many know the other side of the man — Tilak the journalist, the educationist, the scholar and the astronomer. He was instrumental in founding two newspapers in the pre-independence era — the *Mahratta* (in English) and the *Kesari* (in Marathi), as also the New English School in Pune. Both newspapers continue to be published even today from Pune and have a modest circulation.

The Lokmanya also achieved fame when he started a revivalist movement by using the already established forms of Ganesh worship and the Shivaji festival. He utilised both these platforms to impart teachings to the masses and rally them against the British. A champion of the downtrodden people, Tilak had many admirers and was lovingly given the sobriquet 'Lokmanya', which means admired by the people.

Thus, no one can afford to really ignore the impact Bal Gangadhar Tilak had on Indian history. Tilak's life is a story of the beginning of one of the first battles against British rule in modern India, it is a saga of the first stirrings of a people's movement.

Chapter One

Sharp Mind, Iron Will

It is said that a child's most impressionable age is between seven to fourteen years. But, in these years, 'Bal' (young) Tilak in turn, also managed to leave a stamp on the minds of his parents and teachers. The latter certainly had a trying time managing Bal.

Coming, as he did from a lineage of scholars, the young Tilak had no patience for textbook education. So sharp was his mind, that often he would blurt out the answers to the most difficult exercises in Mathematics, even before his teacher had completed the question! This used to upset his teachers who thought Tilak was a bit cheeky. They sometimes insisted that Tilak write down the problem in his notebook before solving it in his mind. Tilak's response was, "Why? I can solve it in my mind."

Another time, Tilak showed early signs of intolerance to injustice when the class teacher decided to punish the entire class for the misdemeanour of one unidentified student. When it

The house in Ratnagiri, Maharashtra, where Tilak was born

was Tilak's turn to be caned, he refused to extend his hand, reasoning that he had not committed the mistake and hence he could not be punished. An astonished teacher then asked him to identify the erring student, but Tilak refused to do that either.

Another example reveals the teenage Tilak's iron will. Once, after passing his matriculation examination in 1872 and enrolling for his B.A. studies with the Deccan College in Poona, he decided to devote an entire academic year only to building a healthy physique!

Till then, Tilak had always been of average health and even sported a slight potbelly. The youngster was sometimes ridiculed for his physical appearance. Also, by this time he was married and his wife, Tapibai, was physically 'better' than Tilak himself. This, too, earned him a lot of scorn. Not a man to take such things lightly, Tilak took it up as a personal challenge and decided to take a course in bodybuilding.

He joined a gymnasium and also learnt Indian style wrestling and swimming. He went on a strict diet comprising vegetables, fruits and wholesome wheat. Morning and evening, for twelve months, Tilak stuck to this regime till he had developed a robust physique. But, he failed in his first year examinations.

Much of Tilak's early education and thinking was moulded, largely, by his grandfather Ramchandrapant and, to some extent, by his father, Gangadharpant. In fact, the first seeds of nationalism were, most probably, planted by the stories that Ramchandrapant narrated to a young Tilak, who sat listening with rapt attention, under a mango tree by the sea. His grandfather had been a witness to some of the inspiring deeds of fearless Indians during the Indian Mutiny of 1857. Gangadharpant, on the other hand, coached Tilak in mathematics and trigonometry at home.

Thus, education, in one way or the other, was Tilak's constant companion. His experiences in college, while completing his B.A. and later, his L.L.B, made Tilak realise the importance of local initiative and enterprise in establishing private schools, modelled on the lines of the English missionary schools. Both he and a dear friend, Gopalrao Agarkar started discussing and thinking on these lines.

The young strapping Tilak's initial shaky step into the limelight was via public education. At least the first eleven years of his public life were devoted to the spread of English education in India.

The 'Lokmanya' with wife Tapibai

Tilak with contemporaries and friends

In 1879, Tilak came in contact with a famous teacher Vishnushastri Chiplonkar. The latter had started a monthly Marathi journal called *Nibhandha Mala* and was among the first to use Marathi effectively to arouse the Marathi-speaking readers.

Between Tilak, Chiplonkar and his other friends, Gopal Ganesh Agarkar and G.M. Namjoshi, they saw the inauguration of the New English School in Pune on January 1, 1880. In a sense, this was the first step in Tilak's journey into public life. The underlying thought in starting the

New English School was education for Indians by Indians. The New English School soon became popular and by 1885, it had over a thousand students.

Later, Tilak moved the main proposal for changing the status of the New English School from a private body to a public institution, to be called the Deccan Education Society. It was also agreed that the trustees of the new board would now work towards founding a new college the following year.

The then Governor of Bombay, Sir James Fergusson, had already expressed his support for the ideals of the members by announcing a donation of rupees one thousand two hundred & fifty when he had visited the school the previous year. Immediately after the news of the new Society was published, the retiring Viceroy of India, Marquis Ripon, also enrolled himself as one of the patrons in December 1884. By that year-end, promises of rupees seventy-five thousand had been secured for the college fund.

The trustees unanimously decided to name the college after Sir Fergusson. Thus, Poona's famous Fergusson College was born. Tilak and most of his friends were teachers here. While Apte was the Principal, Agarkar taught History and Logic, and Tilak, Mathematics.

Some years later, though, Tilak resigned from the Society following a disagreement with some members. The latter wanted to supplement their incomes by doing other work. But Tilak wanted all such members to add their extra earnings to the Society's common kitty. He maintained that the members had taken a vow of poverty and thus, had no right to earn outside. In his resignation letter dated December 15, 1890, Tilak wrote that he had always considered 'self-sacrifice and self-negation' as essential to the success of an educational institution.

वर्गणीचे दर.

सालीना अगाऊ, १

फुटकळ अंकास अर्धा आणा.

वर्गणी आल्या खेरीज अंक

सुरू केला जाणार नाहीं.

केसरी.

जाहिरातीचे दर.

सोळा ओळी किंवा त्याचे

आंत एक रुपया

दुसरे खेपेस निम्मे आकार पडेल.

व्यापारी लोकांचे सोईकरि-

तां अव्वाहिदा ठराव करण्यात

येईल.

स्थिति नो रे दध्याः क्षणमपि मदांधेक्षणसखे गजश्रेणीनाथ त्वमिह जटिलायां वनभुवि ।
असौ कुंभिभ्रांत्या खरनखरविद्रावितमहा—गुरुग्रावग्रामः स्वपिति गिरिगर्भे हरिपतिः ॥

वर्ष १. पुणें:—मंगळवार तारीख ४ जानेवारी १८८१. अंक १.

आज मुंबई इलाख्यांत इतकीं मराठी वर्तमानपत्रें निघत असतां व या शहरांत ही तीन चार चालत असतां, नव्या वर्तमानपत्राची काय जरूर आहे हा विचार आमच्या वाचकांच्या सकृद्दर्शनीं मनांत येणारा आहे. यास्तव प्रथमतः या पत्राचा उद्देश लोकांस कळविणें अवश्य आहे.

वर्तमानपत्रांचा प्रघात पडल्यास आज वीसपंचवीस वर्षे जरी होऊन गेलीं, व गेल्या दहापंधरा वर्षांत तर त्यांच्यांत जरी पुष्कळ सुधारणा झाली, तरी अद्याप वर्तमानपत्रकर्त्यांस आपणांवरची जबाबदारी पुरतेपणीं कळूं लागली आहे, किंवा लोकसुधारणेस आपल्या परिश्रमांनीं केवढें साहाय्य होणारें आहे याविषयीं त्यांचा पक्का समज झाला आहे, असें सामान्यतः पाहतां आढळणार नाहीं. दोन चार नामांकित वर्तमानपत्रांखेरीज बाकीच्यांची जर स्थिति पाहिली, तर वर्तमानपत्र म्हणजे जागोजागच्या बातम्या प्रसिद्ध करण्याचें साधन याच्या पलीकडे वरील शब्दाचा अर्थ पत्रकर्त्यांच्या मनांत कधीं ही येत असलसें वाटत नाहीं. अलीकडे तर लहानसान गांवांतून सुद्धां वर्तमानपत्रें निघूं लागलीं आहेत. छापखाना घालणें व पत्र काढणें हा एक व्यापारच बनल्यानें ज्यास विद्येचा विशेष संस्कार नाहीं अशा मंडळीच्या हातींच वरील दोन अमोलिक साधनें पडलेलीं बहुधा आढळतात. [illegible] खरें आहे कीं, कोणत्याही तऱ्हेनें का होईना, [illegible] दोन साधनांची वृद्धि ही एकंदर देशास श्रेयस्करच आहे. निदानपक्षीं लोकांत वाचण्याचा प्रघात तरी [illegible]ण्यास वरील साधनांचा उपयोग आहे. पण याच उद्योगांत वरच्या पेक्षां चांगली मंडळी पडली असतां लोककल्याणाचा मार्ग ज्यास्त खुला होणार आहे हें [illegible]पष्ट आहे.

वर्तमानपत्राचा मुख्यतः दोन प्रकारांनीं मोठा उपयोग आहे. एक हा कीं, त्यांनीं आपलें काम निःपक्षपातपणें व निर्भीडपणानें बजावलें असतां सरकारी अधिकाऱ्यांवर मोठा दबदबा राहतो. रस्तोरस्तीं रात्रीं दिवे लागलेले असल्यानें व पोलिसांची गस्त सारखी फिरत असल्यानें जो उपयोग होत असतो, तोच उपयोग या कामीं वर्तमानपत्रकर्त्यांची लेखणी सदोदित चालू असल्यानें होत असतो. सरकारी अधिकाऱ्यांनीं आपापलीं कामें चोख रीतीनें चालविलीं असतां त्यांत प्रजेचें किती कल्याण असतें हें कोणास सांगावयास नकोच. पण वरील चोखपणा राहण्यास त्यांचा सर्व कारभार जेव्हां लोकांच्या नजरेसमोर वरच्यावर येत जाईल तेव्हां राहणार. सर्व गोष्टी सर्वांच्या समक्ष होत असल्या म्हणजे अर्थातच लांचलुचपत वगैरे जे अन्यायाचे प्रकार एरवीं होण्याचा संभव असतो तो पुष्कळ अंशीं नाहींसा होतो. जुन्या एतद्देशीय संस्थानांतून वरील प्रकार किती चालत असे, व अद्याप किती चालतो, हें क्षणभर लक्षांत आणलें असतां पत्रकर्त्यांची गस्त लोकांस किती हितावह आहे हें कोणाच्याही लक्षांत आल्या वांचून राहणार नाहीं. विलायतेंत खुद्द महाराणी साहेबांपासून व मुख्य प्रधानापासून तो अगदीं लोक्या सरकारी कामगारापर्यंत सर्वांच्या कारभाराकडे लोकांची नजर वर्तमानपत्रांच्या द्वारें सारखी लागून राहिलेली असते, त्यामुळें कोणता ही अन्याय प्रायः छपला जात नाहीं, व यामुळें तेथील लोक पृथ्वीवरील इतर राष्ट्रांहून सुखी आहेत ही गोष्ट सर्व प्रसिद्धच आहे.

तर सरकारी अधिकारी आपापलीं कामें कोणकोणत्या तऱ्हेनें बजावतात याविषयीं केवळ निःपक्षपातबुद्धीनें व कोणाची भीड न बाळगतां मजकूर लिहिण्याचा आमचा इरादा आहे. अमुक अमुक गोष्ट आहे तेव्हां त्याच्या विरुद्ध कामें लिहिलें, किंवा सरकारानें अमुक अमुक गोष्ट केली तर [illegible]

The first issue of 'Kesari' which was published on January 4, 1881

The scene in 'Gadre Wada' in Pune, (where the college was temporarily housed) was poignant and emotional, to say the least. Tilak had resigned, and the other members recognised the enormity of the moment. A wistful Tilak looked around the room, but he was so wrought by emotions that he could not bring himself to say goodbye. He walked out of the room for the last time with tears flowing down his face. Covering his face, Tilak walked away, an unbent, uncompromised man.

In his initial years of public life, educating people was obviously Tilak's primary motto. But, he realised that while formal education in the classroom moulded the impressionable minds of youngsters, another medium, such as newspapers, was needed to help in moulding the thinking of the masses.

Tilak's emphasis on mass education sprang from the notion that nothing could ever be achieved, not even freedom, without support at the grassroot level. Very briefly, he was taken up by the ideas of Wasudeo Balwant Phadke — the man who raised the banner of an armed revolt against the British in Poona. But the Lokmanya, always a student of history, understood that a renaissance movement was the need of the hour before any revolution could be started in India.

Journalism soon became Tilak's instrument for mass education. He decided to launch two newspapers — the *Kesari* in Marathi and the *Mahratta* in English. While the *Kesari* (The Lion) primarily addressed the masses and tried to eradicate their ignorance, the *Mahratta* was aimed at the slightly more advanced sections of Indian society and discussed high politics. It also offered readers articles from other Indian and foreign journals.

Both the papers were launched in 1881 and met with almost instant success. *Kesari* achieved the highest circulation for any vernacular newspaper in the country by 1882 and the *Mahratta,*

The 'Lokmanya' with his wife and three daughters

too, soon became a powerful newspaper in western India. Even today, *Kesari* is published from Pune and has a modest circulation while *Mahratta* is an annual magazine.

From the beginning, both the newspapers became known for their bold and fearless editorial stand and writings. Nothing was sacrosanct for the publications — from the domination of the British in India to social causes like the woes of Hindu widows. The *Kesari* and the *Mahratta* had an opinion on every subject. Contrary to belief, though, Agarkar was the first Editor of *Kesari,* not Tilak.

For almost his entire public life, Tilak used the newspapers very effectively, not only to educate, but also to put across his forthright views to the masses. Like the Lokmanya's own forceful personality, his brand of writing, too, was full of fire and brimstone. He did not mince words while stating a point. This ushered in a new era in Indian journalism.

Tilak would always dictate his editorials and articles. Many of them, thus, read like public speeches. This suited him, since most of his readers felt as if he was addressing their hearts and mind directly. He was not only an editor but also a philosopher and a guide to them. He wrote in a lucid enough style that the common man could understand. By his writings in the *Kesari,* Tilak truly proved that the pen was mightier than the sword.

Not only was Tilak an astute journalist, but also an author who picked up the toughest subjects and explained them in an easy-to-understand form. Tilak's two works, *Orion* and the *Arctic Home in the Vedas,* are even today hailed as being well researched. In these two works, he proved beyond reasonable doubt that the *Vedas* went back nearly five thousand years B.C. and that the original Aryans came from the North Polar region which was habitable at one time. His third book, *Gita Rahasya,* written in lucid Marathi, is a socio-political thesis based on the most sacred book of the Hindus and was first published in 1915.

Chapter Two

Jai Ganesh! Jai Shivaji!

The shrewd politician that he was, Tilak clearly realised the value of mass support in the campaign for liberation from British rule. Knowing that any immediate constitutional agitation against the British was futile, the Lokmanya wanted to first awaken the common man and educate him in the ways of the British and then let the agitation snowball into a critical mass. This would ultimately lead to the removal of the British from Indian soil.

What also spurred him on in this direction was the general degradation in the lifestyle of the average Indian. Tilak realised that the educated youngsters in the country were only interested in getting employment in the government. The English speaking Indian prided himself in imitating his 'masters', the British, in all ways and mannerisms.

Tilak felt extremely pained by this 'copying' of the British lifestyle. Such Indians had to be rescued from their depths of moral degradation. He thus decided to revive mass movements in

Chhatrapati Shivaji Maharaj

Maharashtra, with the aim of regaining the lost dignity of a people and restoring their self-esteem.

In 1893, Tilak found a suitable platform to launch his revivalist movement in the Ganesh festival. It became the ideal engine to spread knowledge to the masses. Till then, the Ganesh festival in Maharashtra was a mere personal religious occasion being celebrated at home in a low-key manner. Tilak called upon his fellow Maharashtrians to give Ganesh Chaturthi a more community aspect and celebrate it with public fervour.

Under the Lokmanya's inspiration and guidance, devotees all over the region started celebrating the Ganesh festival for ten days with great pomp and fanfare. People would gather every evening before the idol of the Lord and Tilak's followers would shrewdly use the platform for mass propaganda. They spoke on religious subjects and Tilak, a scholar of the ancient Hindu epics, used these themes to underline his speeches.

To use religion to address and discuss the political and economic issues of modern India was a well thought out strategy, used quite successfully against the British. The latter had a 'hands off' policy where religion in India was concerned. Thus, the ten-day Ganesh festival served as a dual edged weapon to educate the masses and also promote Hindu solidarity. By 1896, it had caught the public imagination and more than fifty centres in Poona itself were celebrating the festival.

Having successfully aroused the masses by organising the Ganesh festival, Tilak now turned his attention to creating community leaders. He was a firm believer in the idea that any community could only flourish and prosper as long as it produced leaders capable of leading the masses, of serving their communities. When a society failed to throw up such men, it decayed and then died.

Ganesh festival

Tilak realised that the ordinary man must be given a public figure to hero worship and who better than Chhatrapati Shivaji Maharaj, the founder of the Mahratta Empire. To lakhs of people, he was the ideal hero, the ideal king. Thus, Tilak decided to organise yet another annual festival in Shivaji's honour.

In Shivaji, Tilak felt, he had found that ideal public idol who both the Brahmins and the non-Brahmins would worship. The Mahratta king was also very popular with the youth and Tilak

was banking on their support. In 1895, at a public meeting in Poona, Tilak announced a decision to raise a fund to rebuild Shivaji's crumbling memorial at Raigad. Thousands of followers, including descendants of Shivaji's lieutenants, attended this festival at Raigad Fort. They spoke of those heroic days and Shivaji's achievements and soon, this became an annual event.

The Shivaji festival did not limit itself to the boundaries of Maharashtra. Even in Bengal, which history showed had suffered at the hands of the Mahrattas, it caught the imagination of the people. While addressing a Bengali audience in 1907, Tilak said Shivaji was born at a time when the whole nation required relief from misrule. Shivaji also respected the religious beliefs of the Muslims but had to fight against the tyranny of Mughal rule that had become intolerable to the people.

The Lokmanya then asked the people, more so the Muslim brethren, not to fall prey to the British canard of the Mahratta hero being 'anti-Muslim' and asked the masses to embody his ideals and spirit. "Times have changed and the Mohammedans and the Hindus are in the same boat, so far as the present political conditions of the people are concerned," he said.

By 1906, the Shivaji festival had travelled to Calcutta, Karachi and Madras. In a sense, the two festivals catapulted Tilak into being considered a national leader whose popularity had now reached the four corners of the nation.

To say that Tilak often got into trouble with the British because of his free, frank and fearless brand of journalism, would be an understatement. *Kesari* and *Mahratta,* the two newspapers became highly effective instruments in Tilak's efforts to expose the British administration's ineptness in handling situations. One such occasion presented itself in 1896, when India witnessed a brutal famine and the British simply chose to look the other way.

Tilak wrote many scathing articles in the *Kesari,* where he warned that the farmers were bound to rebel against authority if adequate steps to tackle the famine were not taken soon. The articles questioned why the villagers were dying when the Government continued to hold large sums of money as part of the Famine Insurance Fund? The Lokmanya also extolled the Government to operate the Famine Relief Code.

Through his writings, Tilak managed to rouse thousands of helpless farmers, who were scouring the countryside for tiny morsels of food. Slowly but surely, the spirit of resistance was awakening in the souls of the people and Tilak was convinced that this would soon turn into a nationwide movement for independence.

The British government, realising that things were spiralling out of control, decided to take action, but, not the type that Tilak wanted. Instead of helping the starving farmers, the administration arrested some of Tilak's supporters.

Tilak had another cause on his hands the very next year (1897), when bubonic plague broke out in Poona. A hitherto unknown disease in India, it started in late 1896 in Bombay and spread to Poona. Around four hundred people died in less than four weeks due to this dreaded disease.

The British government realised that bubonic plague was highly contagious and decided to tackle it on a war footing. It appointed an officer of special duty for the purpose, Officer Rand. The latter took the words 'war footing' almost literally.

Rand and his band of soldiers would walk into any house even randomly suspected of having the plague, showing scant respect for Indian customs and habits. They even walked into the prayer rooms without a moment's hesitation. Anybody even remotely suspected of being infected, was segregated and sent off to camps. Families were separated blindly.

Soon, Rand and his team's high-handedness earned the ire of Poona's residents. Allegations that the soldiers were ill-treating women and old men surfaced. Helpless, but enraged, citizens watched from the sidelines as the soldiers carried on with their tasks. They once again looked towards Tilak for direction.

Week after week, the Lokmanya wrote about the inhuman treatment meted out by Rand and his men. He made it clear that he was not against better sanitary and hygienic conditions, but Rand's methodology could not be tolerated. He asked Rand and his men to show a little more common sense while doing their jobs. He even took a citizen's deputation to the officer to explain the public resentment following Rand's oppressive measures.

On June 22, 1897, the diamond jubilee of Queen Victoria's accession to the throne was being celebrated with a dinner party at Government House in Poona. Rand and his equally hated lieutenant Ayerst were shot dead while they were returning from the celebrations. The assassin and his accomplices fled into the night.

Before dawn, the C.I.D. was combing the lanes and bylanes of Poona for the killers. One of them reached Tilak's residence early in the morning and apprised him of the night's events. Even to him, says his biographer, it was evident that Tilak had no inkling of the killing. Incidentally, Tilak too had participated in the celebrations but told the officer, "I had not seen anything unusual."

Poona was placed under curfew. An enraged Government thought that Tilak had some role to play in the Rand murder. They suspected a conspiracy, with the Lokmanya being the moving force behind it. Obviously, Tilak's writings in the *Kesari* had, to some extent, formed this view. The British also announced a reward of rupees twenty thousand for anyone providing a clue to the identity of the murderer.

The lure of money was enough for one of the killer's acquaintances to betray the killer. He turned out to be Damodar Chaphekar. He was put on trial and sentenced to death. Till the very last, Chaphekar insisted that he had acted on his own to avenge the indignities heaped on the people of Poona.

The British government, however, remained unsatisfied. It started viewing every Brahmin leader with suspicion. High on the list was Tilak. While Tilak deplored the murder, he came out with two scathing articles in the *Kesari* headlined, *Has the Government Lost its Head?* and *To Rule is Not To Wreak Vengeance,* in which he deplored the senseless and oppressive measures of the Government.

Though the Government was unable to prove any connection between Rand's murder and the Lokmanya, anti-Tilak newspapers, especially the Anglo-Indian press, started publishing editorials and articles insinuating a plot. Soon, there was an air of mistrust and the Europeans refused to speak to the locals.

Tilak wrote spirited articles against this prejudiced view of the Anglo-Indians and the English editors. In one article he wrote, "It is a great pity that one man's thoughtless action should make the Anglo-Indian community forget the endless forbearance the citizens of Poona had shown in the most trying days..."

This series of articles in the *Kesari* became the proverbial last straw on the camel's back. The Anglo-Indian press in Bombay became more shrill in its criticism against Tilak. Faced with such public pressure, the then Governor of Bombay, Lord Sandhurst, had to order Tilak's arrest.

Apparently, certain evidence, available then, indicated that Lord Sandhurst was initially not in favour of Tilak's prosecution. Not only was he hesitant in ordering the prosecution, but, almost around the same time, he also sanctioned Tilak's election to the Legislative Council for a second time. But since the clamour for Tilak's head was becoming more strident, the Governor had to finally order Tilak's arrest for seditious writing.

In one of his articles, Tilak tried explaining the difference between sedition and resistance: "To create or lead peaceful opposition to foreign rule and to rouse a spirit of resistance is not sedition; true sedition is to incite people to armed rebellion in order to secure independence or the redress of a wrong. If anyone follows the line of direct incitement to violence, then it is sedition and it is the duty of the Government to punish such people. But to inflict punishment indiscriminately on the guilty and the innocent alike is certainly atrocious."

Despite the C.I.D.'s repeated efforts to somehow establish a connection between Rand's murder and Tilak, it was unable to do so. The government prosecutor then, charged him with publishing two seditious articles — one an alleged poem signed with the pseudonym, 'Bhawani Talwar' and the other, a report in the *Kesari* on Tilak's speech defending the killing of Afzal Khan by Shivaji. Both the articles were seen as an incitement to violence.

The first sedition trial against Tilak began in the Bombay High Court on September 8, 1897, before Justice Arthur Strachey and a special jury of nine — six Europeans and three Indians — and lasted six days.

Justice Strachey refused to buy the defence counsel's submission that the article was just a discussion of the ethics of Shivaji's act in killing Afzal Khan. While summing up, the judge referred to this and other lines in the poem and said: "According to the Crown, the suggestion is that amongst the means to be adopted, and which are justified by the great end in view, is political assassination or the destruction of your enemies in any way you think fit... If foreigners are in possession of the country and you cannot drive them out of it, destroy them in it... The

The cell in which Tilak was imprisoned in Yerwada Central Jail, Poona

sentence on the face of it is in the present tense and justified a particular course of action in the circumstances stated."

The judge, however, agreed with the prosecution that there was no case to prove any connection between the articles on the plague and Rand's murder. The six Europeans on the jury found him guilty while the three Indians found him not guilty. Tilak was sentenced to eighteen months' hard labour.

The observations of the judge were later interpreted by many, including legal luminaries, to be almost directing the jury to find Tilak guilty for his writings. Justice Strachey also came in for a lot of flak, many times from even British newspapers, for distorting and misinterpreting certain provisions of the Indian Penal Code.

A special appeal filed in the Privy Council in London against the Bombay High Court judgement failed, and Tilak had to serve twelve of the eighteen month sentence before he was released from the Yerwada jail in Pune.

During Tilak's imprisonment and convalescence, *Kesari* was edited by his two lieutenants, N.C. Kelkar and K.P. Khadilkar. On his release, Tilak once again took control of the paper as editor in July 1899 and in his very first article he wrote: "Despite the new situation now created (by the novel definition of sedition) we are determined to continue to work for the attainment of our objective (swaraj)."

Internment, it seems, was no deterrent for Tilak. If anything, it gave him fresh impetus to write many more such articles.

Chapter Three

Firebrand Politics

"The powerful agitation against the Partition of Bengal had thrown up many able and aggressive leaders of this type in Bengal but the real symbol of the new age was Bal Gangadhar Tilak from Maharashtra."

Pandit Jawaharlal Nehru, in *Discovery of India.*

The years 1905–1908 saw the Lokmanya shedding his title as a provincial leader and emerging as a major player on the national political scene. During this period, Tilak's brand of politics caught the attention of many a leader and found mass following in a section of the Congress youth cadre. It was in this period that Tilak gave his followers the mantras of *Swaraj* and *Swadeshi,* and also passive resistance, which later went on to become the Mahatma's *Satyagraha.*

Lal, Bal and Pal

Tilak's move to centrestage was sparked off by Lord Curzon's sudden decision to partition the province of Bengal on July 20, 1905. While the British administration maintained that the division had been announced for administrative efficiency, Tilak and many others were sure that there was a hidden agenda behind it. Tilak felt that the Government's true motive in dividing Bengal was to break the growing attempt at national solidarity. It was a fact that the Government had divided Bengal on the basis of religion — Hindus in one part of the province and Muslims in the other. But unlike some of the leaders, rather than despair, Tilak felt that the partition was a god-sent opportunity to forge a unity among Indians like never before.

Tilak now began writing scathing articles in the *Kesari,* criticising the partition and calling for its annulment. At the same time, he also advocated the boycott of British goods. He adopted a two-pronged attack — on the one hand, he asked Indians to come forward and register their protest, on the other, he also gave a clarion call to the Congress leaders to stand shoulder to shoulder with their kith and kin in Bengal.

It was during this time that the Lal, Bal and Pal front emerged on the national scene. Two well-known leaders of that era, Lala Lajpat Rai and Bipin Chandra Pal, along with others, joined Tilak's cause. Under Tilak's leadership, a new form of national unity began to be

forged, and he realised that it was time to demand self-government. Thus *Swadeshi* became the slogan of the day.

Now, Tilak was totally submerged in politics, and looked to the Congress to provide him with a platform to espouse his views. He also felt that the Congress party was merely a paper tiger and wanted it to be more pro-active. With political backing from leaders like Lajpat Rai and others, Tilak proceeded to Benares to attend the Congress Session of 1905, presided over by Gopal Krishna Gokhale. On his very arrival at the Benares Railway Station, in front of a ten thousand strong crowd, he gave the slogan: "Militancy, not Mendicancy." This set the pace for the Benares Congress Session.

Tilak's brand of politics, and his exhortation to Congress leaders to not merely pass written resolutions but to follow them up with action, sent flutters

Gopal Krishna Gokhale

Lajpat Rai

down the rank and file of the Congress party. Soon, the delegation from Punjab led by Lala Lajpat Rai and the Bengal delegation led by Bipin Chandra Pal echoed Tilak's new slogan of *Swaraj*. Even the Congress President, Gokhale, in his presidential address, agreed with some of Tilak's views. But the Lokmanya had misjudged the situation and his initial optimism was misplaced. When he wanted Congress to pass an anti-partition resolution to back Bengal's agitation, Gokhale demurred.

A similar tussle revolved around the resolutions relating to the boycott of British goods and the promotion of *Swadeshi* and national education. Though the principles and ideals which they stood for were agreed upon and the reworked resolutions passed unanimously, Tilak had to compromise and tone down the wording of the resolution.

Tilak and his firebrand politics was bound to lead to some sort of a divide within the Congress. Many in the opposite camp thought Tilak was taking an extreme stand. But the youngsters in the Congress and many from the Punjab and Bengal cadre were fast accepting Tilak as their leader.

The Lokmanya now created a fresh chapter in the history of the Congress by introducing a new theory — that of 'passive resistance'. He first expounded on this plan at an open session of the Benares Congress. In Lala Lajpat Rai's own words, this was to achieve a three-pronged goal: "To awaken the masses and liberate them from the 'hypnotic' spell of the British rulers, to create a love for liberty and a spirit of sacrifice for the nation's freedom cause, and finally, to gain independence."

The following year, Tilak elaborated on passive resistance in a lecture at Calcutta, where he laid down the tenets of his New Party. Here, the Lokmanya took pains to explain that: "We are not armed and there is no necessity for arms, either." Tilak pointed out that he and his

Uttarpara, April 1908. Sri Aurobindo (far right), Bipin Chandra Pal (far left)

followers had a stronger weapon in the form of a total boycott. Tilak also outlined what he wanted his followers to do. He asked them to refrain from helping foreigners to rule India. He asked the crowds not to assist the British in fighting beyond the frontiers of India and desist from helping them in collecting revenue. The Lokmanya also asked them not to pay any taxes.

Tilak's passive resistance programme and his Calcutta speech not only came as an awakening for the Congress, but, it also launched the 'Tilak era' in the history of Indian politics. It was this very basic principle of non-cooperation and passive resistance which was later taken up by Mahatma Gandhi in the 1930s under the name of civil disobedience and *Satyagraha*.

When the original boycott resolution was passed on August 7, 1905, it was primarily aimed at the British move to partition the Bengal province. But later, in the *Kesari,* Tilak explained the real meaning and scope of such a political and economic boycott. He called for the imposition of such a boycott at the national level and not be limited to a specific issue such as the Partition of Bengal.

Tilak's popularity began spreading further across the nation, especially among the youngsters. This lot wanted Tilak to preside over the Calcutta session of the Congress. Aurobindo Ghose suggested Tilak's name. Other provinces like Punjab soon followed and it looked as if Tilak was set to become the next President of the Congress.

Pherozeshah Mehta

Inevitably, these developments led to some consternation within the top leadership in the Congress. There was a clear divide within the party — the 'Moderates' and the 'Extremists'. Reading that the presidency of the Congress would soon slip out of their hands if the Extremists in the party had their way, the Moderates decided to bowl a political 'googly'. They invited senior leader Dadabhai Naoroji to be the President of the party at the Calcutta session in 1906.

Naoroji, who began his political career as a Liberal decades ago, had very soon turned into a Radical. The 'Moderates' thought that by selecting him, they would achieve a two-fold purpose: they would foil any design to make Tilak the President and once Naoroji assumed the post, he would counsel the spirited leaders in the Congress like Tilak and quieten their spirits.

Dadabhai Naoroji

Obviously, the nomination of the eighty-one year old Naoroji was not opposed by anyone due to his contribution to the freedom struggle. In fact, even Tilak's supporters applauded Naoroji's nomination for he was the oldest and most respected worker in the party. But contrary to the Moderates' expectations, Naoroji had other plans!

The Calcutta Congress was the largest political gathering ever to be held so far. Over 1,800 delegates had gathered from across the country and over ten thousand people attended it on a daily basis. The presidential speech, though couched in sober and parliamentary language, was full of dynamite. Once and for all, from a public platform, the Congress president declared that self-governance or *Swaraj* was the new mantra.

This declaration thrilled Tilak and the followers of his New Party, but came as a rude shock to the Moderates within the party. Tilak's firm views on how *Swaraj* ought to be wrested from the British and how the Congress ought to conduct its affairs also ruffled many feathers within the party's rank and file. Some even debunked his 'Constitutional Agitation' theory.

There was a verbal duel between the Moderates and the Extremists over the exact wording of the resolutions to be passed at the Calcutta Session. For some time, it looked as if the National Congress would split, much to the delight of the British. But ultimately, an astute Tilak handled the situation in such a manner that the party presented a united picture to the outside world.

On his return to Poona, Tilak wrote several articles in the *Kesari,* praising the decision taken by Dadabhai Naoroji to give a definite lead to the Indian freedom struggle. "Dadabhai, the venerable priest of patriotism, has joined in holy wedlock the National Congress and India's right to Swaraj," wrote Tilak in one article.

A charged-up Tilak now started making plans to turn the *Swadeshi* (boycott) programme into a national movement. The stage was inevitably set for a confrontation between the Moderates and the followers of the New Party. The

Moderates, led by leaders like Sir Pherozeshah Mehta and Gokhale, were trying their best to prevent the country from following the lead given by Naoroji.

A war of words broke out between Tilak and some of the Moderate leaders. In one of his speeches, Sir Mehta explained his stand, saying he believed in "divine guidance through the human agency". He said: "I accept British Rule… as a dispensation so wonderful, a little island set at one end of the world establishing itself in a far continent as different as could be, that it would be folly not to accept it as a declaration of God's will."

The difference between the Moderates and the Extremists was that while the former were prepared to wait for as long as it took to attain their ideal of colonial self-government, the followers of the New Party wanted *Swaraj,* by which they meant complete independence, immediately.

In early 1907, Tilak sparked off fresh debate by penning three articles in the *Kesari* expounding further on his theory of 'Constitutional Agitation' in India. He tried to show the vital difference between the concepts of legal and constitutional agitation and demonstrate how his programme of passive resistance was the only one suitable for India.

While joining issue with Tilak on his constitutional agitation plan, Gokhale delivered a series of lectures in February 1907 at Allahabad, trying to show the futility of passive resistance as advocated by Tilak and his New Party.

In short, although the Moderates and the New Party members differed little in their ideals, their means for achieving the end were quite different from each other. The latter firmly believed that it was impossible to gain any concessions by petitions and prayers. As Tilak argued, "There was no instance in history of one foreign nation ruling another for the benefit of the other and not for its own profit."

It was in an atmosphere of conflict and rebellion that the next session of the Congress was planned. Initially, an attempt was made to hold the meeting in Nagpur but had to be aborted following rowdy scenes. The election of a president was thwarted on a technical point. Perhaps, sensing that the Congress was headed for a split, Tilak offered to step down from the race and instead suggested the name of Lala Lajpat Rai. The Moderates, on the other hand, led by Sir Mehta, proposed the name of Dr Rash Behari Ghose as their candidate. In all this, the Moderates resorted to political machinations and managed to shift the venue of the Congress session from Nagpur to Surat.

The annual session of the Congress party at Surat in December 1907, has gone into the history books as the one where this august body split for the first time ever. Acrimonious scenes were witnessed here. Some Congressmen, including the Lokmanya, were even manhandled by some angry members. From the very beginning, there was hectic backroom activity in both the camps. The Moderates tried to scuttle the boycott resolutions passed in the Calcutta Session, and the Extremists decided to fight this.

The party reception committee at Surat issued a press release stating that there was no move to renege on the previous resolutions. In the meantime, a draft copy of the Congress Constitution that had been prepared by Gokhale had features which if accepted in toto, could exclude nationalists from the Congress. Tilak and his party members decided to launch an agitation against this.

The first attempt to elect the new President on December 26, 1907, ended in an adjournment. A commotion broke out in the *pandal.* Dewan Bahadur Ambalal S. Desai had proposed the name of Dr Rash Behari Ghose as the new President. He was followed by Surendranth Banerjea, who was shouted down and not allowed to speak. All attempts to maintain decorum failed and the meeting was adjourned.

With Nationalist leaders at Surat, December 1907, (From left — front row) Ganesh Srikrishna Khaparde, Ashwini Kumar Dutt; (middle row) Sardar Ajitsingh, Aurobindo, Lokmanya Tilak, Saiyad Haider Reza; (back row) Dr. Munjee, Ramaswamy, K. Kuverji Desai

When the adjourned meeting began the next day, Tilak sent a reminder to the chairman of the reception committee, Tribhuvan Das Malvi, saying that he wanted to address the delegates after the election of the President had been seconded as he (Tilak) wanted to move an adjournment with a constructive proposal. But Tilak's request was ignored. Consequently, after Dr Ghose was taken to the President's chair, Tilak climbed the dais and turned to the delegates to make an appeal to them. He insisted that Dr Ghose had not been 'properly elected'.

This led to riotous scenes as young Moderates in the party tried to pull him down. Tilak stood his ground, though, Gokhale climbed up to the stage to intervene and threw his arms around Tilak. In the pandemonium, a shoe flew through the air and hit Surendranath Banerjea and Sir Mehta. There was

Tilak with colleague Dadasaheb Khaparde

complete mayhem after that, as groups carrying sticks went around the hall and missiles flew everywhere. Thus, December 27 marked the blackest day in the history of the Congress. The hall was soon deserted.

Aurobindo presiding over a meeting at Surat, December 1907. Lokmanya Tilak is addressing the gathering.

Some leaders within the Congress like Motilal Ghose and B.C. Chatterjee tried for reconciliation. They managed to get a letter from Tilak on the morning of December 28, which said that Tilak and his band of followers were ready to accept Dr Ghose as the new President in the best interests of the Congress, provided that the previous year's resolutions on *Swaraj*, *Swadeshi* and national education were adhered to and each expressly reaffirmed. But there was only silence from the Moderates even after this letter. They carried on with their convention and thus, the Surat Session ended in a split within the Congress.

Chapter Four

Tilak and Home Rule

Between 1907–08, the Government of India launched a fresh wave of repression across the country. It implemented a ruthless policy aimed at subverting the leader from the reactionary as well as the constitutional camps. It passed a clutch of laws to curb 'unlawful' activities. This included the Prevention of Seditious Meeting Act, the Explosive Substances Act, the Newspapers (Incitement to Offences) Act. The latter gave power to a District Magistrate to confiscate the printing press of any newspaper, which in his opinion contained an incitement to acts of violence.

Action was initiated against Indian editors. Many newspapers carrying anti-partition reports were placed on the black list by the Government of Bengal. The first paper to come under this was *Bande Mataram* edited by Aurobindo Ghose. He was charged with seditious libel.

Expectedly, Tilak's writings also came under scrutiny. Especially those articles written after the Bengal Partition in 1905, when a picric acid bomb, aimed at Sessions Court Judge Kingsford at Muzufferpore, unfortunately missed its intended target and, instead, took the lives of two British women — a Mrs Kennedy and her daughter.

Tilak had written several articles in the *Kesari* countering the views expressed in English newspapers. Without supporting the violence, Tilak had written spiritedly and appreciated the youthful exuberance of the revolutionaries from Bengal. He had drawn parallels between the bomb attack and the situation in Russia where people were agitating against Czarist tyranny.

Additionally, Tilak had now begun warning the British that the suppressive measures it had recently adopted could backfire, the passage of the Newspapers Act was an attempt to stop the process of awakening, therefore it was possible that the disappointment could take on a more terrible form, he said.

The Governor of Bombay at that time, Sir George Clarke, had these and the other articles which had appeared in the *Kesari* earlier, translated into English and it was not long before it was decided that Tilak would be prosecuted under the two sections of the IPC for seditious writings. Tilak was charged with: "attempting to bring into hatred and contempt and exciting or attempting to excite disloyalty and feelings

Bande Mataram

Weekly Edition.

PUBLISHED EVERY SUNDAY.

Price One Anna. Price One Anna.

VOL. I. CALCUTTA, SUNDAY, SEPTEMBER 29, 1907. NO. 18.

OUR PICTURE GALLERY.

SJT. AUROBINDO GHOSE.

Front page of Bande Mataram Calcutta, September 1907, after Aurobindo's acquittal in the Bande Mataram Sedition Trial

Mohammed Ali Jinnah

of enmity towards His Majesty and the Government established in British India."

The last charge was based on Tilak's last article, *The Country's Misfortune.* Not satisfied with serving a warrant on the basis of just one article, yet another was served based on his article titled *These Remedies Are Not Lasting*.

On June 24, 1908, Tilak was arrested. Even though issued four hours earlier, the British delayed serving the arrest warrants till late evening in order to ensure that Tilak did not get a chance to seek bail. The next day, when his counsel moved court for bail, it was immediately rejected. In July, when Tilak's counsel, Mohammed Ali Jinnah, moved a fresh bail application in the court of Justice Davar, an Indian judge, it was rejected once again. Ironically, it was a younger Davar who had represented Tilak as a barrister in 1897 in his first sedition trial. He had used almost the same arguments as Jinnah did to secure Tilak's bail at that time.

Hearing in this second sedition trial began in July. The special jury consisted of seven Englishmen and two Indians this time. Tilak pleaded his own case. He cross-examined many of the witnesses including the official Government translator who had translated the writings from Marathi into English. At the end, Tilak addressed the jury for over twenty-one hours, over more than three days. The jury took an hour and a quarter to return its verdict — guilty, seven against two.

Justice Davar sentenced Tilak to six years deportation observing: "It seems to me that it must be a diseased mind, a most perverted mind that could say that the articles which you have written are legitimate weapons in political agitation. They are seething with sedition; they preach violence; they speak of murders with approval..."

In reply, Tilak responded: "All I wish to say is that in spite of the verdict of the jury, I maintain that I am innocent. There are higher powers that rule the destiny of things and it may be the will of providence that the cause which I represent is to prosper more by my suffering than by my remaining free." Tilak was fifty-three when he was sentenced.

This time, Tilak's sentencing sent waves of resentment and anger through many sections of society. Thousands gathered outside the High Court to catch a glimpse of the Lokmanya before his deportation. One of the biggest workforces in Bombay, the cotton mill workers, perhaps in anticipation, had already started resorting to sporadic strikes by the time the judgement came in. Some policemen were stoned. The cloth, freight and sharemarkets also closed down immediately after the verdict. The general uproar sent government officials scurrying into a defensive mode.

Newspapers, in both India and Britain, and several public representatives condemned the sentence. The *Mussalman,* the mouthpiece of the Muslim community wrote: "If it was the intention of the Government to give the accused a fair trial, we think the jury should not have been constituted in the manner in which it was. We think his Lordship has gone too far in inflicting such a heavy punishment."

In such an atmosphere, Tilak was taken from the shores of India to the Central Jail of Mandalay in Burma, where he spent the next six years in near-solitary confinement. Another freedom fighter, Subhash Chandra Bose, who was also imprisoned for sometime there, had said that

Pandit Madan Mohan Malaviya

the climate at Mandalay was 'unhealthy' and 'unfavourable to a degree' and more so as: "we ourselves were the inmates of a wooden cage in Mandalay Jail as was Lokmanya Tilak."

Winters were bitter and summers extreme. Until midnight, the air was hot and the place was so stuffy that sleep was impossible, recalled Tilak after his release. Tilak's diabetes fluctuated, sometimes rising to dangerous levels. Age was also finally catching up with the man. He lost five or six teeth while in jail and his hearing became harder.

One of the few concessions allowed by the British to Tilak, besides permission to wear his normal dhoti and shirt, was the availability of books. The British government, though, gave no quarter, in reducing his jail term. It only deducted one month out of the six-year sentence.

The year 1916 was quite an eventful one in Tilak's political career, after he was released from jail. Not only did he form his much cherished Home Rule Movement, he was also welcomed back into the Congress in the Lucknow Session.

Both Gokhale and Sir Mehta passed away in 1915. The death of two of the foremost leaders of the Moderate lobby was seen by some as the crumbling of the last of the opposition to Tilak. This faction predicted an easy re-entry of Tilak into the Congress fold. Tilak, on the other hand, was more cautious. He realised that following the deaths of the two leaders, the remaining Moderates would resist his return till the very end.

Soon, at a Provisional Conference meeting, Tilak made his first major political speech since his release from Mandalay Central Jail. In it, he gave the people a new slogan — 'Home Rule'. This was the only cure for India's political ills, Tilak said.

The First World War was being fought around this time. Tilak realised that this was the right time to seize some of the initiative from the British. He was convinced that Britain would have to rely on India for its vast manpower and other resources in case of a prolonged war. The British Government, on the other hand, was taken aback at Tilak's new Home Rule slogan. They did not want any agitation at such a crucial juncture.

A committee was set up in Madras to examine the desirability of amending Article 20 of the Congress Constitution in order to recommend Tilak and his men to rejoin the party. While Tilak personally was ready to rejoin the Congress, a section of the Nationalists had doubts. Tilak discussed this with his followers in a two-day debate but when a vote was polled, it went against him. The majority did not want him to rejoin the Congress.

The Lokmanya held a similar discussion once again at the Bombay Provincial Congress meeting at Belgaum in 1916. The issue was fully thrashed out and he finally rejoined the party. Around this time, the Indian Home Rule League was also formally inaugurated. Tilak felt that the demand for *Swaraj* could be made more effectively by forming such a body.

In his first speech on Home Rule, delivered in Belgaum on May 1, 1916, Tilak made out a strong case for self-government and the people's determination to get it. Tilak clearly stated that the institution of Kingship could not be confused with the bureaucratic administration of India. These were two separate things, he insisted.

"The question of *Swaraj* had nothing to do with the King. Its demand does not involve any sedition. The essence of *Swaraj* is that we manage our own domestic affairs according to our wishes…," he said. Tilak claimed India's right to independence was not only for the material well-being of its people but also for their spiritual and moral well-being.

In July 1916, his followers decided to celebrate Tilak's 61st birthday. Without his knowledge, they planned a grand celebration. On the same day, the Government issued a show cause notice to Tilak and asked him to submit a surety for rupees forty thousand. The reason — the

Government had taken objection to Tilak's speeches in Belgaum and Ahmednagar. The Government felt that Tilak had incited the people to be disloyal to the Government established by law.

Tilak then approached the Bombay High Court against this show cause notice. And Tilak's counsels, Jinnah and Erulaker, were able to show the distinction that Tilak had clearly made between a Government established by law, a permanent institution and the administration which was subject to change. As the personnel of the administration changed from time to time, the nature of their work also changed, they argued. The High Court judges, Batchelor and M. Shaha, accepted Tilak's definition and said the speeches were not seditious. This was a very important victory for Tilak.

On December 28, 1916, the Congress session in Lucknow opened with a standing ovation for Tilak and he spoke on the main resolution of self-government. Tilak also achieved an agreement between the Hindu and Muslim leaders over the question of Muslim representation in Central and Provincial Councils, defeating the machiavellian designs of the British.

Tilak prevailed upon Pandit Madan Mohan Malaviya and Jinnah, the leaders of the opposing groups, to come together and settle this contentious issue. On December 31, he attended the Muslim League session where he was also accorded a standing ovation. Many Muslim leaders congratulated Tilak on his liberal role in pursuing the Muslims to accept the proposals in the Lucknow Pact.

The Lucknow Congress session finally buried the hatchet between the Moderates and the Extremists in the Congress as also between the Hindus and the Muslims. As such, it is seen as a turning point in India's march towards *Swaraj,* Home Rule and Independence.

Chapter Five

End of an Era

One of the most important contributions which the Lokmanya made during the last years of his life was to create an awareness among the British masses about the plight of Indians under British rule.

In early 1918, the Lokmanya sought permission to go to England but was forced to return to Poona after reaching Colombo as the Government of India withdrew the permission. Finally, in September 1918, Tilak was given the go-ahead again and he reached English shores on October 30.

Tilak was in England to attend the hearing of the libel suit he had filed against Sir Valentine Chirol, who had made certain remarks and observations against Tilaķ in his book, *Indian Unrest,* published in 1910. Tilak's contention was that Sir Chirol had damaged his reputation in his book in six different ways. The most damaging and libellous of these statements were

London 1st October
1919

Dear Sir

Please accept my warmest thanks for your kind message of congratulations and good wishes on the occasion of my 64th birth-day. God grant that I may yet deserve it by my work. Believe me

Yours very sincerely

B.G. Tilak

" श्री " लंडन, १ आक्टोबर
१९१९

कृ. सा. नि. वि. माझ्या ६४ व्या जन्मदि-
वसाच्या प्रसंगी आपण स्मरणपूर्वक
जो प्रेमाचा निरोप मला पत्रद्वारे पाठवि-
ला त्याबद्दल मी आपला अत्यंत ऋणी
आहे. त्या प्रेमाला अनुरूप अशी योग्यता
हातून कांही देशसेवा घडून [illegible]
परमेश्वरापाशी माझी प्रार्थना आहे. कळावे
लोभ असावा, हे विनंती. आपला

बाळ गंगाधर टिळक.

A facsimile of Tilak's handwriting

Tilak before leaving for England

the author's observations about the Rand and the Jackson murders vis-à-vis Tilak.

When the book was first published, Tilak was unable to initiate any action as he was serving his six-year sentence in Mandalay. But once he was out, Tilak consulted lawyers in Bombay and London and filed the suit together with an injunction to restrain Sir Chirol and his publishers from publishing the disputed matter. After nearly three years of delay, (some of it because of the war), the case had now came up for hearing in the King's Bench Division in London before Justice Darling and a special jury.

But the verdict by the British jury went against Tilak. The latter, who had till then relied on the British sense of fairplay to get justice, was now shattered. Financially too, he had suffered a major setback while fighting the libel case. He sent orders to sell his assets back in Poona to raise the necessary funds. Soon, however, other important issues preoccupied him.

Coincidentally, he was in England at the time when the First World War had just ended.

(l to r):
George Bernard Shaw ; Sydney Web of the Fabian Society ; Prime Minister Clement Attlee of Labour Government from 1945–1951

Motivated by the mood around him, Tilak decided to start his work on Home Rule. But the Government of India had gagged Tilak by refusing him permission to speak from public platforms in England. His lawyers, referring to a similar case involving another Indian leader, managed to get the order rescinded after applying to the War Cabinet.

Immediately, Tilak started explaining his viewpoint on Home Rule in England. Along with delegates of the Indian Home Rule League, which had arrived in England by then, Tilak appeared before the Parliamentary Joint Select Committee set up to consider the Government of India Bill prepared by Edwin Montagu, Secretary of State for India. He explained his viewpoint in front of this Committee. Tilak's work in England is seen by many as the first-ever serious attempt on the part of India to enlighten the British about Indian affairs.

While in earlier cases, leaders such as Dadabhai Naoroji and G.K. Gokhale had tried to put across their views in a select influential circle, Tilak realised that it was the British masses, the real source of power in a democracy, who he had to address. He was the first leader to approach the British people through their own newspapers and organisations. Tilak began attending Labour Party conferences, Trade Union Congress meetings and those of various other worker parties. He launched a full-scale public movement to garner support for Indian Home Rule and India's right to self-determination.

Soon, Tilak grew close to the British Labour Party. The latter reciprocated and assured him that the Independent Labour Party would give him the support he needed. Tilak subscribed to the funds of the Labour Party and gave a cheque of two thousand pounds to help turn the weekly *Herald* into a daily newspaper. In turn, the paper reproduced articles strongly supporting the Indian demand for Home Rule and several other such articles written by Tilak and his colleagues.

Tilak had already established the Home Rule headquarters in Adelphi Terrace from where books, pamphlets and manifestos dealing with Home Rule in India started pouring out. Among the other people Tilak met while in England were George Bernard Shaw and Sydney Web of the Fabian Society. Many political observers opine that it was Tilak's overtures to the Labour Party that paved the way for friendship and understanding which ultimately led to the Labour Government, under Richard Atlee, granting complete independence to India in 1947.

On his return to India, the citizens of Poona presented Tilak with a purse of rupees three lakhs to enable him to pay the costs of the libel suit.

They had collected this money over a period of time in response to an appeal published in the *Kesari*. Never before in Indian public life had such a large sum been collected for any leader.

Mahatma Gandhi, presiding over the May 30 meeting, paid a handsome tribute to Tilak saying: "It would be a mistake to suppose that the people's respect and love for him would diminish because of the verdict of the British court... One must admire the Lokmanya's tenacity and courage. Undaunted by legal defeat, he continued carrying on his national work in England. When he is engaged in fighting our battles there, it is our duty to collect funds and relieve him of his financial worry."

Mahatma Gandhi

In July 1920, Tilak suffered an attack of malaria. On Monday, July 26, his fever took a serious turn. The base of his left lung was affected. The *Sardar Griha* in Bombay, where Tilak was staying, was besieged by anxious followers. Leaders of all hues, from Jinnah to the Mahatma, came calling.

On Wednesday, July 28, his heart started showing signs of weakness and on Thursday, he suffered a heart attack. Throughout Friday and Saturday, Tilak remained unconscious. His condition worsened and despite last minute

LAUNDRY

medical efforts to save him, Tilak died at forty minutes past midnight on August 1, 1920. His wife, three daughters, other family members and friends were notified to come and pay their last respects.

The next morning, Tilak's body was placed on a raised chair in a sitting posture. From early morning, enormous crowds gathered to catch a last glimpse of their departed leader. People started arriving in special trains from Poona and the entire area from Crawford Market to Dhobi Talao was filled with the sad mass of people.

Almost the entire citizenry of Bombay, cutting across all sections of society, turned out for Tilak's funeral procession. From the common man to leaders like Mahatma Gandhi and Lajpat Rai — everyone was there. His body was consigned to the flames at Chowpatty at 6 p.m. The curtain thus came down on an eventful era in Indian history.

The last 'yatra'. Tilak's funeral procession in Bombay

Acknowledgements

The author would like to place on record his appreciation and acknowledgement to the 'Kesari Mahratta Trust', Pune, for giving him complete access to archival material and photographs, while researching this book. He would also like to thank Dr D.J. Tilak, General Manager Trustee of the Trust, and also Shailesh Tilak and other staff of the *Kesari,* Pune, for extending their unstinted co-operation. The writer is also grateful to the Trust for providing him with its sponsored, authorised biography of Bal Gangadhar Tilak called *'Lokmanya Tilak — Father of Indian Unrest and Maker of Modern India'* written by D.V. Tahmankar, which helped in the research.

ABOUT THE AUTHOR

Sorab Ghaswalla, News Editor with a leading national news agency, has nearly eighteen years experience as a journalist in a number of well-known national and international publications like *The Times of India, The Indian Express, The Economic Times,* the *Hindustan Times* and *The Gulf Today.* He has the distinction of working in television as well as a dotcom besides his experience in the print media. Also a columnist, he writes on a variety of subjects like politics, crime, education and films.

NOTES

NOTES

15